# HOW TO INVES
# STOCK MARKET
# FIRST TIME AND
# MAKE MONEY
## A STEP-BY-STEP GUIDE

# By Aloysius Yongbi Fontama
M.Ed. MSc. PGCE. BSc (Hons). MCP, MCSE

# About the Author

Aloysius Yongbi Fontama is an **Investor, Private Tutor, Mentor and Founder of A&F Capital Advisors [Financial Education firm]** and **A & F Tutors. A&F Tutors** is an education consulting firm aimed at adding value to people through 1-2-1 **private tutoring, mentoring and coaching.** It also uses education as a tool for **social and economic mobility,** especially those from low-socioeconomic background. **A & F Capital Advisors** is used as a tool to help people, especially those from low socio-economic background with the **knowledge, tools and skills** required to acquire **financial security and freedom.**

**Academic and Career Profile:** After graduating from Cass Business School, City, University of London with a **highly prestigious Quantitative Finance and Financial Engineering course, - MSc in Mathematical Trading and Finance,** Mr Fontama spent a few years in various analyst roles as an **Investment, Special Projects and Trading Floor Technical Analyst in Private Equity and Investment banking sectors.** Through his experiences in Investment Banking, which included teaching and training other staffs, Mr Fontama discovered his twin passion to make a positive transformation in people's lives and sharing knowledge to empower people. This explains why he wrote this book i.e. **to empower people with the knowledge and skills** required to help them in their journey to **financial security and freedom.**

Currently, **Mr Fontama is studying towards a PhD in Personal Finance Education.** He also a Master's degree in Education, BSc (Hons) in Chemistry and Chemical Processing Engineering, including Microsoft Certified Professional and Microsoft Systems Engineering Certifications [MCSE].

For more information on private tutoring, mentoring, financial education, apprenticeship and career mentoring services, please visit our website **www.aandftutors.com** or contact us at **admin@aandftutors.com.**

"Sometimes it is the journey that teaches you a lot about the destination" – Drake

# ACKNOWLEDGEMENTS

First, this book is dedicated **to God the Almighty, who gave me the strength, knowledge and wisdom** to put it together.

Secondly, I dedicate it to my mother **[Bibiana Aghigha Yongbi] and late father [Godfrey Chiambeng Yongbi]** who taught me the value of education and sacrificed all they had to ensure my siblings and I had the best education they could afford.

Third, my gratitude goes to **all those who have made a positive impact on my life [in particular, my late cousin, police inspector, Njua Julius] whom I never had the chance to say, Thank You,** for your unconditional support during the most challenging period in my life.

**May this book be a financial blessing in your journey to financial security in Jesus name.....**

## RISK WARNING

o Materials in this book can be used **for training and education purposes only** and **cannot** be used as **financial advice.**

o Also, the value of your **investments can go down as well as up and you may get back less than you originally invested.**

o So, it is important you understand the **risks involved in investing before investing your money.**

o If you are unsure, please consult a suitably qualified financial adviser.

o Past performance is not a guide to future performance and some investments need to be held for the long term.

# Table of Contents

*"Long term investors must hold stocks even though the market is risky, because they are still likely to produce better returns than alternatives"*

*John Bogle [Founder of Vanguard]*

## CHAPTER 1: WHAT IS A STOCK? WHAT IS THE STOCK MARKET?

- A stock is a piece of a company, the more stock you purchase the more of the company you own,
- The stock market is a place where stocks and bonds are bought and sold.

### *Types of stocks*

- Common Stocks: This is stock offered to general public and you get dividends for owning the stock
- They carry risk of bankruptcies
- On the contrary, preferred stocks pay fixed dividends, but carry limited risk because holders are paid first in case of bankruptcies before common stockholders.

### *Why Invest in the Stock Market?*

- Stocks are good investment because they allow you to own part of companies that have proven to be successful over long periods of time, which you would not be able to own otherwise.
- Therefore, it enables you to own part of a business or a whole business, just like having a share or equity in your own home, which explains why **stocks** are sometimes called **equities.**
- **Why own stocks**? In most cases, the quickest way to become rich is by owning something through investment, be it stocks, bonds or business or property.
- For example, **Andrew Carnegie, Roman Abramovich, Philip Green, Steve Jobs, Warren Buffet, Jeff Bezos, Mark Zuckerberg**, and the founders of Google and other multimillionaires and billionaires have only been able to become rich, **moneywise,** by owning **100%** or part of their companies i.e. becoming shareholders.

- **Passive Income:** Owning stocks enables you to create passive income [money earned with little or no effort], lets your money be your "slave" by working hard for you, rather than you doing the hard work.
- **Owning stocks helps you** make money through **appreciation** of your capital i.e. capital gains and **through dividends.**
- **Capital appreciation** means profits made after buying and selling a stock. For example, you buy a stock of Apple for $100 or £100 and sell for $120 or £120. This means you have made a profit of $20 or £20, assuming you have **subtracted the transaction cost of the trade.**
- However, note, although the goal is capital appreciation, the value of your stock may reduce too (depreciate). For example, I bought **Tesla [please see symbol TSLA in figure 1 below] stock in October 2018** hoping it will increase in value **[capital appreciation]**

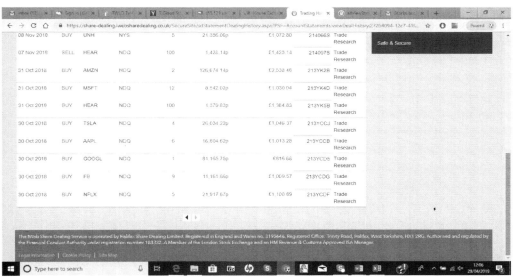

Figure 1

- By 29/04/2019, that is 6 months after buying the stock, TSLA's stock price dropped by **30.42% [please see figure 2 below to confirm]** due to regulatory, political risks and to an extent ineffective leadership from management.
- **United Health Group (UNH)** had similar losses

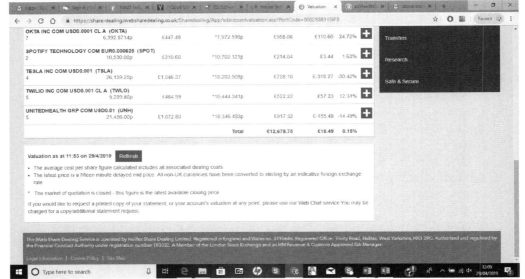

Figure 2

**Lessons from this case study 1:**

1. **Although** investing in the stock market **can be very profitable long term, it is also risky,** because the value of your investment may **either go up or down.**

2. When it goes down, it means you may get back less than what you originally invested.

3. Having said that, you could make significant profits over the long term if you buy good quality companies because **of capital appreciation [we discussed it earlier], dividends and compound interest.**

4. **The best way to explain why you should invest in the stock market is seen in the case study below**

5. **This case study carried out by top stocks analyst from one of the best stockbrokers – Motley Fool, explains how if you could have turned $1000 into $1000,000 by investing in the 3 top quality stocks in the stock market – with dividends reinvested.**

# 3 Stocks That Turned $1,000 Into $1 Million

*These are prime examples of why it pays to invest early in high-quality, founder-led companies.*

Billy Duberstein
(TMFStoneOak)
Jan 2, 2020 at 9:16AM

*"If investing feels rather intimidating, don't let that stop you from starting, or at least beginning to learn how. That's because over the long term, equities, on average, are almost certain to appreciate, and they grow much faster than inflation rises. Keeping your savings in a bank -- especially at today's rock-bottom interest rates -- is almost certain to erode your wealth due to inflation. For a stress-free retirement, you'll need to invest early and often.*

*If you're intimidated by trying to pick stocks yourself, fear not. You can choose from many actively managed mutual funds and low-cost passive index funds that can give you diversified exposure to a broad index of equities.*

*However, it can also pay to invest a portion of your savings in individual stocks, because winning growth stocks can go on to beat the broader market by staggering amounts. In fact, investing in one of the top stocks in the world at a relatively early stage has the potential to fund your entire retirement.*

*Don't believe me? Here are three examples of stocks that turned just $1,000 into a cool million bucks -- and even more.*

### Amazon

*In perhaps the greatest feat of modern business, e-commerce and cloud computing giant Amazon.com (NASDAQ:AMZN) has turned $1,000 into more than $1 million in just 22 years as a public company. Founded as an online bookseller by Jeff Bezos in the early days of the internet, Amazon has expanded its reach into virtually every aspect of the consumer and business economy. From books, the company went on to offer a much wider range of goods and services, with as much depth of inventory, value, and delivery speed as possible, in order to delight customers.*

*In an unconventional turn, Amazon's management decided to eschew dividends or buybacks after the company's initial success. It chose instead to reinvest all profits back into the business: building more infrastructure, extending the company's first-mover advantages in e-commerce, and inventing new products and services.*

*These have led to several huge businesses, including the Prime subscription program that now offers free one-day shipping and access to Amazon's award-*

winning Prime Video catalogue. Amazon is now also becoming a threat in digital advertising, a segment that's expected to exceed $11 billion in revenue for the company this year.

But the most consequential Amazon "invention" is Amazon Web Services. By developing a way for companies to outsource their computing and storage needs to Amazon's hyperefficient data centers, AWS pioneered the cloud computing revolution, which is disrupting the highly profitable enterprise computing and software spaces. From a standing start in the mid-2000s, AWS is now a business with a run rate of $36 billion, growing at 35%, and with operating margins between 25% and 30%.

Amazon has been able to achieve and maintain this success by adhering to the business principles set forth in Bezos' first 1997 letter to shareholders: He preached focusing on the long term rather than short-term profits, not being afraid to experiment, and obsessing over customers above all else.

The results? After going public in 1997 at $18 per share, Amazon.com split its stock three times (twice 2-for-1, and once 3-for-1), for a split-adjusted IPO price of just $1.50. At today's stock price of roughly $1,850 per share, that equates to a return of 123,200%, turning $1,000 into $1.23 million today.

### Microsoft

The other cloud computing giant besides Amazon is **Microsoft** (NASDAQ:MSFT), another company that's turned $1,000 into more than $1 million. Of course, the cloud wasn't Microsoft's primary business. After its founding in 1975 by Bill Gates and Paul Allen, Microsoft's first winning product was an operating system for the earliest personal computers.

Microsoft later released its flagship product, the Windows operating system, in 1983; it would go on to sell Microsoft Office, the dominant software suite for all kinds of business tasks, beginning in 1989. Subsequent releases included the Internet Explorer web browser in 1995, the Xbox video game system in 2001, and the Microsoft Surface laptop and tablet in 2012.

However, Microsoft's most consequential modern product is its Azure cloud computing service, now a strong No. 2 to AWS in the cloud computing space. The cloud unit was helmed by executive Satya Nadella, who assumed the CEO role in 2014 and has led a renaissance in Microsoft's growth prospects ever since. Nadella also led the acquisition of LinkedIn in 2016, a purchase that looks savvier by the day, putting the leading business-oriented social network under Microsoft's corporate umbrella.

Though Microsoft initially went public in 1986 at $21 per share, the stock has split many times, and its split-adjusted IPO price is a mere $0.072 (just over seven cents). That means at today's share price of around $157, Microsoft stock has appreciated 217,900%, turning $1,000 into $2.18 million over 33 years.

## Berkshire Hathaway

Finally, let's look at **Berkshire Hathaway** (NYSE:BRK-A) (NYSE:BRK-B), the financial conglomerate founded by Warren Buffett. The company got its start when Buffett, a successful investment-fund manager, took a controlling stake in declining New England textile business Berkshire Hathaway in 1964. Fortunately, Buffett and partner Charlie Munger soon realized the textile business had subpar long-term prospects; they pivoted, taking the cash flow from Berkshire and diversifying into the insurance business.

Buffett and Munger then took the insurance "float" -- premiums received before liabilities have to be paid out -- and used their value investing skills to buy shares of high-quality equities and to buy entire companies outright. This was an innovative, and slightly riskier, way to invest insurance float, which traditional insurers usually put into lower-risk bonds.

However, Buffett and Munger, two of the best investors of all time, picked several gigantic winners over the subsequent years and decades. These included GEICO and See's Candies, both of which Berkshire now wholly owns; **Coca-Cola** in the 1980s; several highly profitable bank investments after the financial crisis of 2008; and even a foray into technology, with a successful 2016 investment in **Apple**.

Not only do Buffett, Munger, and Buffett's two lieutenants Todd Combs and Ted Weschler invest the float from Berkshire's large and diverse insurance operations -- but under the guidance of insurance head Ajit Jain, most of Berkshire's insurance operations themselves are quite profitable, even before investing the gains. This combined team and business model has allowed Berkshire's market value to compound over 20% annually for 55 years, a stunning achievement for that amount of time and for a company so large. These gains have enabled Berkshire Hathaway's stock to increase roughly 2,700,000%, turning a mere $1,000 investment in 1964 into a stunning $27 million fortune today.

### What made these stocks big winners?

*What are the common characteristics of these incredible winners? All three companies were founded and run by bona fide geniuses: Buffett, Bezos, and Gates. Those geniuses were also master capital allocators, aggressively reinvesting most of their profits to further strengthen their business moats, and then creating new high-return businesses -- some quite different from their companies' original products or services.*

*After all, Windows is now an afterthought for Microsoft investors, who are more focused on Microsoft's cloud and other software products. Many Amazon investors think most of the company's value is now tied up in AWS, third-party services, and advertising, not its original direct e-commerce operations. And Berkshire Hathaway shut down its textile operations in 1985, keeping only the name of the original mill.*

*Thus, the right formula for massive investment gains seems to be: Identify geniuses with the right business models, and the freedom to reinvest in new businesses and services as they see fit; have the faith to hold your money with them over the course of years and decades.*

*Of course, there aren't many business geniuses out there with the right open-ended business opportunities. But if you think you've found one, don't hesitate to invest. As these three companies have shown, a small investment can go a very long way.*

*https://www-fool-com.cdn.ampproject.org/c/s/www.fool.com/amp/investing/2020/01/02/3-stocks-that-turned-1000-into-1-million.aspx*

## Lessons from this case study

- Investing in **good quality companies with effective leaders** early enough, who ensures that the company **stays innovative and reinvest its profits wisely by creating products or services which increase profits or acquiring other companies that add share holder value** leads could generate massive returns over the long term

- Secondly, **reinvesting dividends paid by these companies, combined with the power of compound interest** generates higher returns than compared to when dividends are not reinvested.

# What are Dividends, Compound Interest, and Time value of money?

- Besides capital appreciation of stock price, some companies pay dividends.
- A dividend is an additional payment you earn because you own the company's stock i.e. this comes from the company's profit, and the company decides the amount **every quarter after earnings e.g. after recent earnings, Lockheed Martin** [a global security and aerospace company] declared a dividend of $2.20 per share.
- **Why Companies pay dividends?** Dividends may be used as a way of increasing demand for shares which are not performing well or convincing existing shareholders to keep the stock and reinvest dividends which helps you to generate better returns on investment in stocks compared to bonds and cash.
- **But every investment needs "Time" to appreciate or increase in value because "Time" is a friend of investment.**
- This explains why you need understand what "Time value of money" means.

**Time Value of Money**

- Stock market has returned **about 11% a year for the past 75 years**, compared to **bonds which returned 3.3%,** with inflation growing at about 3%.
- "Equity (and bond) investments have historically outperformed cash over the long term. The average annual return on UK investments between 1989 and 2014, adjusted for inflation, is 5.2% for equities, 4.6% for bonds and -0.8% for cash." **(Morningstar, Inc., and M&G, as at 30.11.14).**

- **This shows that every investment needs time to increase [ in case of good investments] or decrease in value [ for bad investments]**

- However, although **cash offers very little potential for growth or income, it is less risky than equities or bonds**. While there is no limit to how much an equity investment can grow, **there is also no limit to how much it can fall.**

- **This is another reason why equities are best held for the long term to increase your chances of beating inflation and increase the value of your stock or portfolio, assuming you have bought good quality companies.**

- This means investing in stocks may help you to **beat inflation,** whilst increasing purchasing **power of your money** – your ability to afford more things.
- **Therefore, if you intend to live longer than 10 years, you need to invest in stocks**.
- You may also get money from the stock you own in the form of dividends –sums of money paid to investors quarterly as benefit of owning that stock- piece of company profit.
- **Sources of Income:** Owning stock could give you two income streams: **income from capital appreciation and dividends**
- Owning stocks or shares of **good quality** companies could increase  the value of your money by more than **500%** over 5 to 10 years period.
- For example, from **June 2013 to June 2018, Amazon's stock price has increased by 535%, Facebook by 750% and Netflix by over 1000%** as shown in figure 3 below:

## CASE STUDY 2

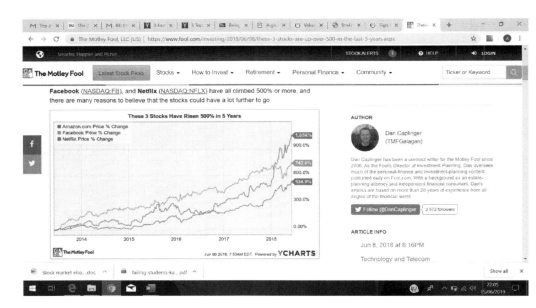

Figure 3 [Online] Available at:
https://www.fool.com/investing/2018/06/08/these-3-stocks-are-up-over-500-in-the-last-5-years.aspx.[Accessed on 15/06/2019].

- More so, other non-technology companies have **produced gains of over 500% over an 8 year period from 2009 to 2017** as seen in figures 4, 5 and 6 below

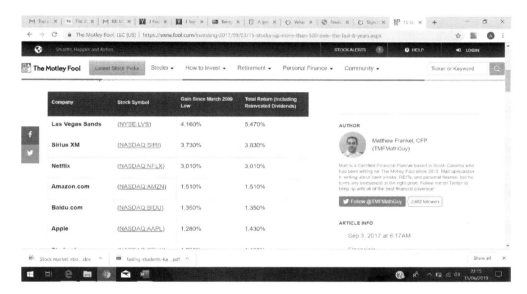

Figure 4

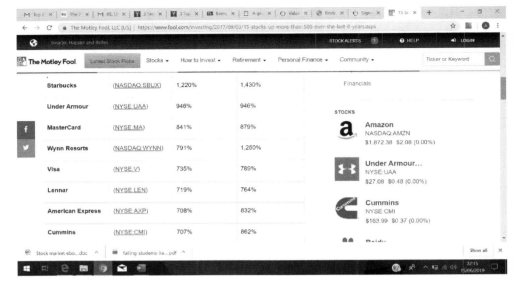

Figure 5

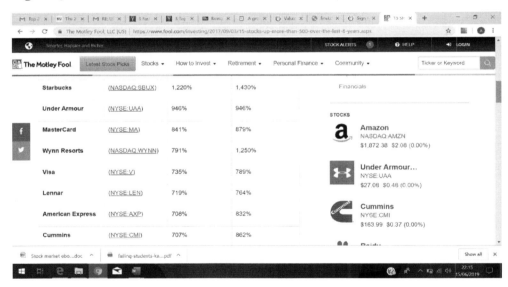

**Figure 6** For detailed information on this please visit
https://www.fool.com/investing/2017/09/03/15-stocks-up-more-
than-500-over-the-last-8-years.aspx.

## LESSONS FOR CASE STUDY 2

- To make significant profits or gains from stock market investment, you must **be ready to buy good quality companies and hold them for a long time.**

- **Warren Buffet, one of the most successful investors in the stock market confirmed this in the following words**:

- *"Investing is a long game, he says. "I know what markets are going to do over a long period of time: They're going to go up. But in terms of what's going to happen in a day or a week or a month or a year even, I've never felt that I knew it and I've never felt that was important," Buffett told Becky Quick on "Squawk Box" in February 2016. "I will say that in 10 or 20 or 30 years, I think stocks will be a lot higher than they are now." Buffett has also likened buying stocks to owning more tangible assets. "If you own stocks like you'd own a farm or apartment house, you don't get a quote on those every day or every week," Buffett told "Squawk Box." So, too, should it be when you're buying a share of a company."*

- Hopefully, now you understand **why investing in the stock market is one of the best investment decisions you could have ever made**, if you pick the right stocks **and investing in good quality companies [I will explain later how to identify these companies].**

## Compound Interest

- The stocks above performed so well partly due to compound interest which I will try to explain below.

1.  If I bought stock Apple shares for £1000 and made 7% average annual rate of return.
2.  This means a year later, my stock value will be £1070 (1000 multiplied 7/100) representing a £70 profit.
3.  Therefore, total stock value at end of year 1 = £1000 + £70 = £1070
4.  Let us assume I do not cash in my profit by selling, but left it for another year.
5.  **That means I will earn another interest of 7% in year 2 on previous interest of 7% in year 1.**

6. **My stock value after two years will be = Year 1 value plus Year 2 value**.
7. Year 2 stock value will be 7% of Year 1 value = 7% of £1070 = 7/100 x £1070 = £74.90
8. **Therefore, total value of stock after two years = £1070 + £74.90 = £1144.90**
9. Hence in Year 1 I earned an interest of £70 but in Year 2 I earned more i.e. £74.90 instead of £70 as in Year 1 due to earning interest of 7% in Year 2 on previous interest of 7% in Year 1.
10. Essentially, I earned more because I reinvested my profit earned in Year 1, enabling me to earn more money in year 2 than in year 1.
11. **Compound interest simply means earning interest on interest**
12. Having seen now that you can make money from the stock market, probably, your next question would be: **where do I buy stocks and how do I buy stocks?**
13. **The graph below demonstrates the power compound interest in stock market investment**

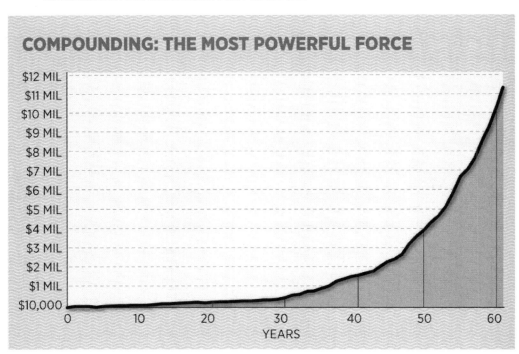

*Power of compound interest: merely adding $200 per month to an initial $10,000 in the stock market over the past 61 years would have produced an $11 million portfolio.*
*SOURCE: INVESTOR.GOV*

**"Compound interest is the eighth wonder of the world",**
**He who understands it, earns it. He who doesn't, pays it"**
**– Albert Einstein**

**CHAPTER 2: WHERE AND HOW TO BUY STOCKS. WHAT ARE STOCK INDICES**

- Stocks can be bought on stock exchanges through a broker [companies who gives access to investors to **stock exchanges** so they can buy and sell stocks or shares]
- Examples of brokers in the UK are **IWEB, AJ BELL, Interactive Investors, Hargreaves Lansdown etc., and in the USA: TD Ameritrade and Charles Schwab in the USA.**
- A stock exchange provides a place for investors to buy and sell stocks
- Examples of exchanges include the FTSE 100 in the UK, New York Stock Exchange
- The FTSE 100 is an index composed of the 100 largest (by Market Capitalisation) companies listed on the London Stock Exchange (LSE).

- These are often referred to as 'blue chip' companies, and the index is seen as a **good indicator of the performance of major companies listed in the UK**.

### What does FTSE stand for?

- The FTSE 100 name originates from when it was owned 50/50 by the Financial Times and the London Stock Exchange (LSE), hence FT and SE makes FTSE. It also references its make-up of 100 companies.

- In the UK, the other FTSE UK indices include the FTSE 250 (the next 250 largest companies after the FTSE 100) and the FTSE SmallCap (the companies smaller than those). The FTSE 100 and

FTSE 250 together make up the FTSE 350 — add in the FTSE SmallCap and you get the FTSE All-Share.

- Similar stock exchanges in America include the New York Stock Exchange (NYSE), NASDAQ, S&P 500

- Another US stock exchange is The **Dow Jones Industrial Average** (DJIA), often referred to as the "Dow Jones" or simply as "the Dow," is a price-weighted average of the stocks of 30 large

- American publicly traded companies. Created by Charles Dow in 1896, it is the most well-known U.S. stock index and is used to gauge the market's performance from day to day.

## *What is a price-weighted index?*

- In a nutshell, a price-weighted index means that higher-priced stocks have more influence over the index's performance than lower-priced ones

## *The current "Dow 30"*

- Here are the 30 stocks that currently make up the DJIA, listed in alphabetical order. (This list was updated in November 2018. **3M, American Express, Apple, Boeing, Caterpillar, Chevron, Cisco Systems, Coca-Cola, DowDuPont, ExxonMobil, Goldman Sachs, Home Depot, IBM, Intel, Johnson & Johnson, JPMorgan Chase, McDonald's, Merck, Microsoft, Nike, Pfizer, Procter & Gamble, Travelers, UnitedHealth Group, United Technologies, Verizon, Visa, Walgreen Boots Alliance, Wal-Mart, Walt Disney.**

## *What is NASDAQ?*

- **Nasdaq** is a global electronic marketplace for buying and selling securities
- It is the benchmark index for U.S. technology stocks.
- The term, "Nasdaq" is also used to refer to the Nasdaq Composite, an index of more than 3,000 stocks listed on the NASDAQ exchange that includes the world's foremost technology **and tech giants such as Apple, Google, Microsoft, Oracle, Amazon, and Intel.**

## *What is the S&P 500 or Standards and Poor?*

- The S&P 500 index is a basket of 500 of the largest U.S. stocks, weighted by market capitalization.

- The index is widely considered to be the best indicator of how large U.S. stocks are performing on a day-to-day basis.

## *Composition of the S&P 500*

- *The S&P 500 consists of 500 large-cap U.S. stocks, which combine for about 80% of all U.S. market capitalization.*
- For this reason, the S&P 500 **is considered to be a good indicator of how the U.S. markets are doing.**

- Examples of stocks in S&P 500 **Apple, Microsoft, ExxonMobil, Johnson & Johnson, General Electric, Amazon.com, Facebook, Berkshire Hathaway (B shares) and JPMorgan Chase.**

## *What are stock brokerage firms?*

- Brokerage firms give investors access to stock exchanges to buy and sell stocks. So, they act as a bridge between the investor and stock exchanges **or the stock market**
- These firms do so by registering with stock exchanges and comply by their rules and regulations

## *Types of Brokerage Firms*

- There are **full brokerage firms** and **discount brokerage firms**
- Full brokerage firms are big investment banks like Goldman Sachs, JP Morgan, UBS, and others
- Avoid full brokerage firms because their commission, fees and/or charges are **very expensive**. It is also suitable for very rich individuals, governments and institutions with the money to afford them
- Discount brokerage firms are more suitable for the average individual investors because their **commissions or charges per trades are much lower.**

## CHAPTER 3: HOW TO CHOOSE THE RIGHT DISCOUNT BROKER FIRM

- Discount brokerage firms in the UK are IWEB, AJ BELL, Hargreaves Lansdowne, The Share Centre, IG share dealing, Interactive Investor
- **Factors to consider when choosing brokerage firms:** The key factors to consider when choosing brokerage firms are **market exposure, platform fees, cost per trade and how easy the platform** is to use in buying and selling shares, etc.
- But considering that your main goal of investing is to make a profit and increase the value of your money, the most important factors amongst these are **cost per trade and "ease of use"**
- **Cost per trade** is the charge you pay every time you buy and sell a stock. **These charges, if not managed well could reduce a huge part of your profits**
- Unlike other discount brokerage firms with higher cost per trade and platform fees, **IWEB is much easier to use, has a "one off" charge of £25 to open an account and a low cost platform which charges £5 each time you buy or sell a share or fund, and has no administrative charges or inactivity charges.**

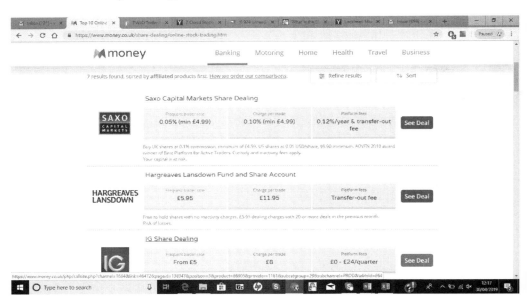

Figure 7

- You can do more **research on other platforms** using these links https://www.money.co.uk/share-dealing/online-stock-trading.htm https://uk.stockbrokers.com/guides/share-dealing-accounts
- Having said that, the key is to **do your research**, taking all those factors into considerations, before making a decision of which broker meets your needs
- For investors in the USA, **the best low-cost platforms to buy and sell stocks are TD Ameritrade, E Trade, Charles Schwab, Ally Invest, Merrill Edge, etc.** You can do more research using the following the links
- https://www.fool.com/the-ascent/buying-stocks/best-online-stock-brokers-beginners/ https://www.investopedia.com/best-brokers-for-beginners-4587873
- **Though the choice of discount brokerage firm depends on the individual, I prefer IWEB due to reasons discussed earlier.**

# CHAPTER 4: HOW TO USE IWEB TO BUY AND SELL STOCKS

Assuming you have read and understood **why you should invest, which platforms to chose and why,** the next step is to open a stock trading account.  For guidance we will use IWEB as an example to demonstrate how easy and straightforward it is to make that **first step to financial security and independence by opening an account.** In summary, the steps are:

1. Go to IWEB Home page by clicking the following link below

2. https://www.iweb-sharedealing.co.uk/share-dealing-home.asp

3. On this page, please click  the **"Learn more"** icon in the IWeb Online Share Dealing box

4. This takes you to the page where you will see the different types of stock accounts offered by IWeb i.e. **Stocks and Shares Isa, Share dealing and Self-Invested Personal Pension (SIPP) accounts**

5. Then Click the **"Apply now"** button at the end of the page, read the information on the page and click the button at the end of page, next to the message *"I understand I will not receive advice and that any investment decisions are my own*

6. Fill in your personal details, where you live and contact details on the next pages

7. Please when you get to the page with the question "**how to invest your dividends**" IF YOU WANT BETTER RETURNS ON YOUR INVESTMENT, PLEASE CHOOSE **"Reinvest any dividends".**

8. Choosing this is a smart way to super charge this process is **take full advantage of the power of long-term investing is by reinvesting your dividends through a dividend reinvestment plan** (DRIP).

9. A DRIP is an automatic way to use your dividends to buy more shares of the stocks in your portfolio

10.    **If you do this, you do not have to worry about it when you buy new stocks – the benefits of dividend reinvestment will begin automatically.**

11. Follow through the wizard to the end and once it is completed, your account is open

12. Usually, once you open stock and shares ISA account on IWeb, a Share Dealing Account will automatically be opened also.

13. Now it is time to fund your account and start trading/investing


## *How do I fund my account?*

1. Please ensure the **bank card you** used in opening your IWEB account will be the one you will use to **fund your account always.** It makes the funding process much easier for you.

2. Be careful not to choose the **share dealing account** when funding your account, because you **pay tax on profits made in Share Dealing Account**

3. Next, **decide how much money you can set aside without worrying about it or thinking of withdrawing for at least 1 year - 5 Years minimum, to maximise the effect on compound interest on your returns.**

4. It could be **5 - 10% of your income** or savings depending on what you are comfortable with e.g. if you earn a £1000 per month or have saved, you can set aside £50-£100 per month.

5. It is entirely your decision, so just make sure you are comfortable with the amount to invest.

6. However, if you have a savings of say £10,000, you could set aside £500 - £1000 per month to invest in the markets – depends on you.

7. Note that your **profits made on your investment will be proportional** to the amount invested. **The same applies in case you lose money.**

8. Once the decision has been made, open your IWEB share dealing account again, **Click "Fund this account" option** in the stocks and shares account

9. Make sure the **"Transfer money in from"** button is **selected [please see figure 8 below]**

10. Type in the amount – On IWeb, you can only transfer a minimum of £2, meaning anything from £2 and above is fine

11. Type in the amount, click **"Continue"** button on bottom right hand corner of the page and the amount you typed in **will be credited into your stock account immediately.**

12. Now you are ready to start investing in the stock market.

13. Perhaps the next real question to answer now is: **How do I buy stocks on this platform i.e. IWeb**

# CHAPTER 5: HOW TO BUY STOCKS ON IWEB

1. Before buying stocks on IWEB or any trading platform, the first **step is to find out if the stock is UK based or international.**

2. To buy a UK based stock such as Tesco, Sainsbury's or Fevertree, Click **"Home button"** on right hand side of the page, then **"Dealing", after selecting your stocks and shares account option**

Figure 9

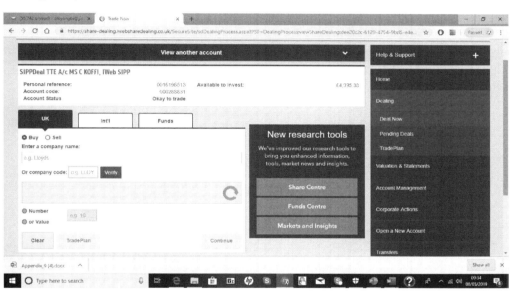

3. Make sure the **"Buy"** option is selected when buying a stock as seen in Figure 9 above

4. But before selecting the buy or sell option, **please make sure the UK tab is selected [by clicking on it]** if the stock is based in the UK or **"Int'l" if the stock is in the USA or another location other than the UK**

5. Type in the name of the company in the row with message saying **"enter a company name" e.g. once you start typing Barclays Bank, it is will come up, then select it.**

6. Click **"Number"** option to indicate the number of shares you want to buy.

7. Once you type in number of shares, the **"Continue"** on bottom right hand corner of the page will be highlighted

8. Click **"Continue"** and complete the process by clicking the **"Deal Now" button as shown below in figure 10**

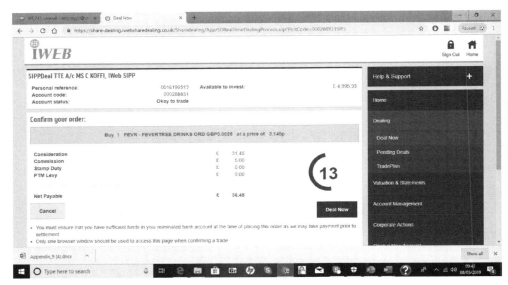

*How do I calculate the number of shares to buy based on share price of the stock at the time and the amount of money I have?*

- Let us assume you have **£100 to invest in Fever tree shares**

- At the time of writing this book, *IWEB's trading policies states that you can only invest **90% of** the amount you have in your stocks account to ensure that your account does not go into **overdraft.***

- This means you will have **£90 available to invest and £10 as reserve in your account – which works out to your favour both in terms of ensuring that your account is in credit and when next you are funding your account, you will have more money to invest e.g.** say you have £10 credit in your account and credit your account with £200 in future, that you will have £210 in total. **10% reserve means £21 credit should be left in your account, implying you have £189 to invest instead of £179 without £10 reserve**

- With £90 to invest, use a **reliable resource to check** the price of the stock at that point in time such as **Google and Yahoo Finance** for all stocks either in the UK or international etc

- **FOR USA STOCKS: If the company is based in the USA, Finviz stock screener is the best place to go for up to date stock price, latest news and research https://www.finviz.com/.**

- To do that, type the company name in the **rectangular box on the top left hand corner of screen** [ with message "search company] as seen below in figure 11

31

- Or in **Google search bar, type "fever tree share price"** and tap "Enter" button on your keypad, and you will see **the latest price of the stock in** the format below

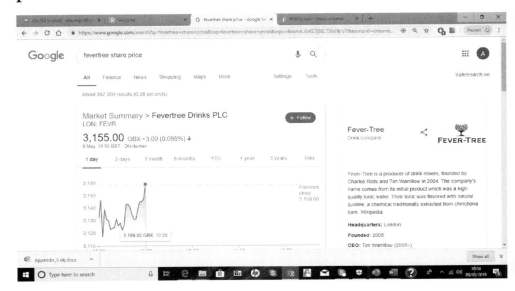

Figure 12

- Because Fevertree is a UK based company, prices are displayed in **pence,** so the price of Fevertree at the point writing this sentence was 3155.00 pence as shown in figure 12 above.

- To know the exact number of shares your £90 can buy, please change this amount to pounds (£) as follows

- 100 pence = £1, Hence, 3155.00 pence to pounds will be 3155 divided by 100 = £31.55 for 1 share of Fevertree

- **Therefore, to know how many shares of Fevertree you can afford with £90, we divide £90 [money available to invest by the price per share = £31.55**

- £90 divided by £31.55 equal = 2.85 shares of Fevertree

- **NOTE: This means in theory, we can buy 2.85 shares of Fevertree but in practice we can only buy 2 shares of Fevertree not 2.85 shares [ 2 and 85/100] because shares are not sold in fractions. Shares do not exist in fractions.**

- Therefore, with £100 you can afford 2 shares of Fevertree, which costs 2 x £31.55 = £63.10

- **This means your total cost for the trade will be £63.10 + £5 [for cost of the trade] = £68.10**

- NB: for US companies, the same process applies to US but please note you will be working in dollars which means you **have to convert your money in pounds to its dollar equivalent.**

*"What an investor needs is the ability to correctly evaluate selected businesses. Note that word "selected": You don't have to be an expert on every company, or even many. You only have to be able to evaluate companies within your circle of competence. The size of that circle is not very important; knowing its boundaries, however, is vital." – Warren Buffet*

*One of the most efficient and efficient ways to achieve a goal is to learn from someone or others who have achieved that goal – a mentor" - Aloysius .Y .Fontama*

*"The fastest way to accelerate your progress is to model and to mentor," Robbins says. "But you have to model and mentor someone who's really done it, somebody who's the best in the world at it, because they know those little two-millimetre differences that nobody else knows." – Tony Robbins*

### *How do I know which stock to buy?*

- As stated above by Mr. Buffet and Robbins, an investor needs the ability to **identify a good quality company and to learn from mentors, to be a successful stock market investor.**

- So what can we learn from some of the masters of stock market investment on how **to identify good quality companies to own their shares/stocks?**

## Lessons from experience

Before passing on Mr Buffet's advice on how to become a successful stock market investor, it is important to note the following about stock market investments from my experience:

- Follow an informed path and conduct your research on the stock you want to buy

- Buying what **news headlines tell you** to buy most often does not work

- Buying what friends, neighbours or relatives tell you to buy does not work either

- But buying the stock which has **the characteristics of a quality stock or company** after thorough research **could lead to significant gains** from your investment in the stock market

- Ultimately, what helped me and what will help you is to study from the masters such as **Warren Buffet, Peter Lynch, Phillip Fisher, Carl Icahn, Ray Dalio and others**.

## *Mr Buffet's Advice on what type of stocks to buy*

- Mr Buffet advices **to buy good quality companies** rather than speculating the about the direction of a **stock price – because prices are fickle**

- Reason being good or quality companies remain good even when times are bad

- When you buy a good company and the price of the stock drops, it is time to buy more shares of the company

- Make sure you understand businesses you invest in – this means you should invest **within your circle of competence**

- For example, with an academic and professional background in technology, **I invest mostly in technology stocks because technology is my circle of competence**.

# HOW CAN I FIND TOP QUALITY COMPANIES? - ANSWER: LEARN FROM THE MASTERS OF STOCK MARKET INVESTMENT LIKE WARREN

## WARREN BUFFET'S ADVICE

**FIRST ADVICE:** The first feature of a quality company is **effective leadership.** Top quality companies have effective leaders who can manage the company well both in good times and bad times

- The **management or leaders** of top quality companies must **be honest** with shareholders and always **act in their interest**

- Reason being integrity is key to business success. **Integrity** means being honest and having strong moral principles

- There is no point to evaluate a business if its leaders are not honest – else you will be evaluating lies.

- **How to check a company's integrity:** Look for clear explanations of the company's successes and failures in its quarterly or annual reports to shareholders.

- This will help you to continuously understand the business you are investing in, what risks you are exposed to and how you can put strategies to manage those risk in case you invest **or to say the least,**

- Enables you to make **an informed decision** of how much risks you are willing to take.


**SECOND ADVICE:** BUY COMPANIES WHICH EARN MORE CASH THAN IS NECESSARY TO STAY IN BUSINESS AND DIRECT THAT CASH WISELY.

- To Mr Buffet, companies that direct money wisely are those what **invest in activities which earns them more money they cost**

- Or companies which **return that money to shareholders in the form of increased dividends or stock buybacks**. With stock buybacks, aka share buybacks, the company can purchase the **stock** on the open market or from its shareholders directly. In recent decades, **share buybacks have overtaken dividends as a preferred way to return <u>cash</u> to <u>shareholders.</u>**

- **Buybacks are used by companies to consolidate ownership, eliminate negative views about the company to increase stock price, make a company look more financially attractive**, and to attract investors as summarised in figure 13 below

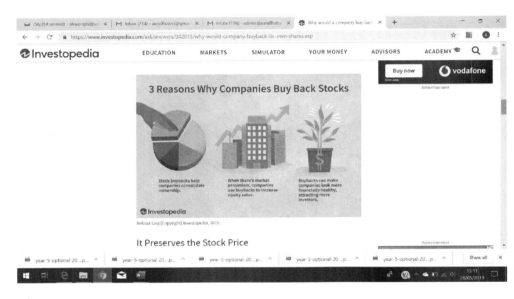

Figure 13

- The best way to identify companies which invest or direct **their excess cash wisely** is by using a financial measure called **RETURN ON EQUITY [ ROE]**

- ROE = NET INCOME DIVIDED BY TOTAL SHAREHOLDER'S EQUITY. IF A COMPANY'S NET INCOME = £8 million, and total shareholder's equity = £ 40 million,

- **ROE = £8 million divided by £40 million = 0.2 x 100% = 20%**

- If a company maintains a high return on equity as it grows, you know that management is directing money wisely

- Though there is no requirement for ROE, ROEs of at least 20% maintained or improved over the years is a good benchmark.

- But value investors will accept negative or lower ROEs in companies they think are about to make a change for the better

- **IN SUMMARY, 20% ROE IS A SOLID RETURN ON EQUITY AND THE BIGGER THE BETTER, THOUGH A STEADY ROE IS GREAT TOO BECAUSE IT SHOWS THE COMPANY CONTINOUSLY RETURNS SUBSTANTIAL PROFITS TO INVESTORS**

**THIRD ADVICE:** BUY COMPANIES WITH HIGH NET PROFIT MARGIN.

- A company's net profit margin [NPM] is determined **by dividing the money left over after paying all its expenses by the amount of money it had before paying expenses.** So if a company makes £1 million and pays £900,000 in expense, its net profit margin is

- NPM £900,000/£1000,000 X 100% = 10%

- Ideally, **buy companies which have net profit margins in the top 20% of its industry. These are the leaders in their field**

- Relative values are better than absolute values because NPMs change from industry to industry

- Ideally, with net profit margin, bigger the value the better.  For example, if you have a company in your portfolio and come across another one in the same industry which is equal in all regards but better NPM, strike off the old one and add new one

- **In summary with net profit margin, bigger is better and if this increases yearly, that is great news**.

**FOURTH ADVICE:** Focus your portfolio on a few good companies because buying a few good companies is better than diversifying across hundreds of average ones.

### Philip Fisher's advice on what stocks to buy

- Philip Fisher is author of the book *Common stocks, Uncommon Profits*. Mr Fisher is founder of a leading investment and asset management firm with 107 billion USD of Assets Under Management [AUM].

- Warren Buffet was so impressed with Mr Fisher's book that he met with him to learn more about his strategies and in 1969, told Forbes, **"I am 15% Fisher and 85% Benjamin Graham**

- **Fisher also agrees with Warren Buffet** that the key to become a successful stock market investor is to **buy quality companies**

- Mr Fisher, just like Mr Buffet, agrees on **buying top quality companies** which have the following characteristics

  - Shrewd management or honest management.

  - Though shrewd management is hard to define, it simply means the company has leaders who are innovative, look past the present to come up with new products in the future which will increase sales and profit

  - Choose companies with increasing sales revenue because sales are key to company growth and prosperity. Sales without profit is useless.

  - Profits must follow sales, and the best way is to examine its profits is to examine its net profit margins

  - As discussed earlier, the company's net profit margin should be 20% and should be maintained or increase yearly

  - The company should be a low-cost producer of its products and services

  - Focus your portfolio on a few good companies because buying a few good companies is better than buying hundreds of average ones

**From the information above, we can conclude that Mr Buffet and Fisher, and other masters of stock market investments like Ray Dalio and Carl Icahn, all agree on the following:**

1. Before buying any stock, ignore the daily minute by minute, daily or hourly changes in the price of the stock and do not speculate the direction of the company's stock price

2. Rather carry out a detailed research of the company to identify if it is top quality company

3. Top quality companies have a decent ROE i.e. 20% ROE, high net profit margins, have shrewd and honest management, do not have too much debt (even better, they do have more cash than it is needed in their reserves

4. Top quality companies also have  good leadership and use cash reserves wisely by increasing dividends, buying back stocks of the company or investing wisely to increase sales, revenue and profit in the future

5. Also, they are innovative to continuously increase their sales, revenue and profit, and stay ahead of their competitors

6. Building a portfolio which is focused on few good quality companies rather buying hundreds of average companies

7. Buy more of the stocks that are performing well.


**WHAT I HAVE LEARNT ABOUT TOP QUALITY COMPANIES OR STOCK – IN OTHER WORDS MY EXPERIENCE**

1. I agree with the Master's that the key to long term successful investment in the stock market is to buy and hold top quality companies with most or all of the **7 characteristics above for the long term**

2. This will help you take advantage of the impact of compound interest [earning interest on interest] as discussed earlier.

3. Moreover, buy stocks with a **"new something" be it a new product or service which is driving the price of the stock to** a **"New High" – New high means the stock has never reached that price before**

4. Research carried out by William O'Neil between 1953 to 1993, founder of *Investors Business Daily*, a competitor of Wall Street Journal, found out that stocks which performed well during this

period had a consistent record of coming up with a new product or service which took its price **to a "New High**

5. For **growth investors, ignore valuations such as Price to Earnings Ratio, but focus on earnings acceleration**.

6. Institutional Ownership: buy stocks which are in demand by institutions because they are the best investors as they buy millions of shares at once. Note, the price of the stock may "sink" when they sell too, so keep an eye on changes in institutional ownership

7. Buy **stocks whose quarterly and annual earnings per share, abbreviated as EPS is accelerating**. In other words, stocks with earnings per share momentum

8. You calculate EPS by dividing what the company earned for the quarter or year by amount of shares outstanding – Though it is easy to find a company's EPS from different sources like Finviz.com below.

Figure 14

[Online] Available at:
https://finviz.com/quote.ashx?t=AMZN.[Accessed on 10/06/2019]

9. As seen in the figure 14 above, Amazon's EPS has been accelerating. It had EPS of 102% in the last 5 years and forecasted to have EPS of 335.7% and 60.6% this year and in the next 5 years, respectively.

10. I have also found out that top quality companies also have other important characteristics

- They are leaders in their sector, so target stocks which are leaders in their sectors

- They have high barriers to entry i.e. they have little or no competitors e.g. **Facebook, Amazon, Google, Netflix, Twilio, Alteryx, Mongobay, Adobe, Okta, Shopify, Visa, Mastercard**

- Also, buy stocks which **have the potential of generating Asymmetric Returns.** This means those that you could invest £1 to make £5 or £10 profit. An example of asymmetric returns can be seen with Facebooks stock performance over the last 5 years as shown in figure 15 below

[Online] Available at: https://www.macrotrends.net/stocks/charts/FB/facebook/stock-price-history.[Accessed on 30/05/2019]

o We can see from the chart above that Facebook's share price was about **$20 in 2012** but today and at time of writing this book, it has risen to **$182.19, equalling a rise of 810.95%**

o This means if you bought Facebook shares in **2012, you would have made more than 8 times the amount you invested in 2013.**

o Another example of stocks with **asymmetric returns is Twilio** which has risen 860% since its **IPO [stands for Initial Public Offering -when a company makes its stocks available for investors to buy in the stock market]** in 2016.

o For more information, please visit https://finance.yahoo.com/news/twilio-takes-advantage-760-surge-213627260.html

o More so, **buy stocks with good social enterprise value.** This means they take good care of their staff and invests in the community.

o **"There is evidence that stocks of companies with good social enterprise value usually outperform those without good social enterprise value" – Wall Street Journal.**

o **Finally, stocks like Twilio may not have decent ROE and Net Profit, but it is still a top quality stock because it is a leader in its sector, have high barriers to entry, shrewd management, sales and revenue has been on the rise since its IPO and has had positive analyst ratings of "Buy" 80% of the time since its IPO**

# SUMMARY – REDEFININING GOOD QUALITY STOCKS OR COMPANIES

From what the masters of stock market investment say and my experience, stocks which exhibit

- **80% of the above characteristics, in particular, those which are leaders in their sector with high barrier to entry,**

- **Have increasing sales, revenue and profit, honest leadership, are innovative and**

- **Those rated as a "Buy" or "Outperform" 70-80% of the time, are top quality stocks to invest in.**

# CHAPTER 6: HOW TO RESEARCH A COMPANY OR STOCK

1. **Registration:** Please register free on various research platforms including Shares Magazine, Motley Fool, Bloomberg, Morning Star, and various Apps such as moneybox **for updates and latest news on your stocks of interests etc**

2. **USA/INTERNATIONAL INVESTORS MOSTLY:** For Investors trading in the US markets **which has proven to generate higher returns than investing the UK or European markets** over the long term, the best place **for free research articles, price changes, stock performance on weekly, monthly, quarterly and yearly basis,** please register free **on finviz.com or bookmark the webpage on your Google Chrome or Explorer browsers.**

3. **Research Approach:** Search the stock on **Finviz.com by typing its symbol or name in the box on top left-hand corner as described**. If using another search engine, type stock symbol **[also called ticker]** in the appropriate box as advised earlier.

4. Choose at **least 3 positive" articles about the stock e.g. stock coming up with new product, latest analyst rating explaining why stock is a "Buy"** to find out why it is a "buy", and recent **quarterly earnings report** indicating that the company's earnings per share, sales, revenue and profit beat analyst estimate. **This is buy signal**

5. Also, choose **3 negative articles why the stock may not be a top quality company** e.g. articles explaining why a **company's chief executive has resigned, analysts rating advising investors to sell the stock or downgrading it or its earnings per share below expectation or** company's management selling off their shares of the company etc

6. Read these articles in **detail, identify reasons why the stock is a "buy" [if the stock has most of the characteristics of a good quality company or "sell" [if it has it is not performing**

well because its risks are more than positives]. **Make detailed notes of these information.**

7. Check at **least two or three other sources to confirm your findings** about the stock.

8. **Then you can make an informed decision whether to Buy the stock of the company or not.**

9. **Usually, Motley Fool articles are very good research articles because they have detailed and comprehensive information on which stocks to buy for short, medium to long term investors and why.**

10.       **Zacks, Bloomberg, Morning Star or Investor place's articles also** have good articles on which stock to buy or sell at over short term, including advice on which to buy before the company declares its earnings report and top stocks in a particular sector.

11.       **FOR USA/OTHER INTERNATIONAL INVESTORS MOSTLY:** Also register on **Seeking Alpha website to create a table of your investment portfolio, monitor daily stock price changes or pre-market changes.** This provides regular and daily updates on stock price movement and recent updates of factors affecting the company's stock price and performance

12. If you can, subscribe **to Wall Street Journal, Shares Magazine and/or Sunday Times** for additional information about investment, and how other factors such as  political risks can affect the performance of your stocks or investment portfolio [a portfolio is the group of stocks that you have bought or put together in your list of stocks]

13. For example, the **US – China trade war has had** a huge negative impact on the entire market since October 2018. Between October and December 2018, it led to huge sell off in global stock markets. Such factors are greater than individual risks linked to a company stock, hence your overall portfolio could drop.

14.       **So please keep an eye on the performance of global stock indexes [ please refer to previous chapter on Indexes] using Seeking Alpha, CNBC, Bloomberg or any other suitable source**

**15.** For more information on how political and economic risks affects the markets such as the USA-China trade war, please read these articles from 3 different sources

- **https://www.theguardian.com/business/2019/may/29/global-markets-fall-as-china-prepares-to-hit-back-at-us-in-trade-war**

- **https://www.ig.com/no/markedsnyheter-og-analyse/trading-opportunities/how-could-a-us-china-trade-war-impact-markets--180328**


**Another frequently ASKED questions during my financial education sessions with investors is:**

**"Where can I go to find out potential good quality companies?"**

- **Answer**: When you read articles about say **Amazon,** usually, these articles will usually talk about Amazon's competitors, which acts as a **lead for further research** and indication of potential good quality companies.

- However, to make the job easier for you, so I thought it was necessary to share this **database of 69 of top 250 most effectively managed U.S. companies according to the Drucker Institute of Management in the USA as a starting point for your research.**

- According to Wall Street Journal, these companies have been ranked based on the following factors: **customer satisfaction, employee engagement and development, innovation, social responsibility and financial strength.**

- **As seen in the list below in Figures 15 - 20,** the table shows that **Amazon as top, Google, Microsoft, IBM, Cisco Systems, Apple , Nvidia, Johnson and Johnson, Procter and Gamble and 3M occupying the top 10 position.**

| OVERALL RANK | COMPANY | SECTOR | OVERALL SCORE | EMPLOYEE | INNOVATION | SOCIAL | FINANCE |
|---|---|---|---|---|---|---|---|
| | Apple Inc. | Technology | 100.0 | ★★★★★ | ★★★★★ [+] | ★★★★★ | ★★★★★ [+] |
| | Amazon.com Inc. | Technology | 99.4 | ★★★★ | ★★★★★ [+] | ★★ | ★★★★ |
| | Microsoft Corp. | Technology | 87.7 | ★★★★★ | ★★★★★ | ★★★★★ | ★★★★★ |
| | Nvidia Corp. | Technology | 84.1 | ★★★★★ | ★★★★ | ★★★★★ | ★★★★★ |
| | Intel Corp. | Technology | 83.7 | ★★★★ | ★★★★★ | ★★★★★ | ★★★★★ |
| | Alphabet Inc. | Technology | 82.7 | ★★★★★ | ★★★★★ | ★★★★ | ★★★★★ |
| | Accenture PLC | Business/ Consumer Services | 82.1 | ★★★★ | ★★★★★ | ★★★★★ | ★★★★★ |
| | Johnson & Johnson | Health Care/ Life Sciences | 81.5 | ★★★★★ | ★★★★★ | ★★★★★ | ★★★★ |
| | Procter & Gamble Co. | Consumer Goods | 79.3 | ★★★★★ | ★★★★★ | ★★★★ | ★★★★★ |
| | International Business Machines Corp. | Technology | 79.2 | ★★★ | ★★★★★ | ★★★★★ | ★★★★ |

Showing 1 to 10 of 252 entries

| OVERALL RANK | COMPANY | SECTOR | OVERALL SCORE | EMPLOYEE | INNOVATION | SOCIAL | FINANCE |
|---|---|---|---|---|---|---|---|
| | PepsiCo Inc. | Consumer Goods | 77.4 | ★★★ | ★★★★★ | ★★★★★ | ★★★★ |
| | 3M Co. | Business/ Consumer Services | 77.2 | ★★★★ | ★★★★★ | ★★★★★ | ★★★★ |
| | Cisco Systems Inc. | Technology | 76.8 | ★★★★★ | ★★★★★ | ★★★★★ | ★★★ |
| | Starbucks Corp. | Leisure/Arts/ Hospitality | 76.2 | ★★★★ | ★★★★★ | ★★★★★ | ★★★★★ |

| OVERALL RANK | COMPANY | SECTOR | OVERALL SCORE | CUSTOMER | EMPLOYEE | INNOVATION | SOCIAL | FINANCE |
|---|---|---|---|---|---|---|---|---|
| 15 | Nike Inc. | Consumer Goods | 75.8 | | ★★★★ | ★★★★★ | ★★★★ | ★★★★★ |
| 16 | HP Inc. | Technology | 75.7 | | ★★★★ | ★★★★ | ★★★★★ | ★★★★★ |
| 17 | DowDuPont Inc. | Basic Materials/ Resources | 75.5 | | ★★★ | ★★★★★⁺ | ★★★ | ★★★ |
| 18 | General Electric Co. | Business/ Consumer Services | 74.2 | | ★★★ | ★★★★★⁺ | ★★★★★ | ★★ |
| 19 | Clorox Co. | Consumer Goods | 73.9 | | ★★★★★ | ★★★ | ★★★★★ | ★★★★★ |
| 20 | United Parcel Service Inc. | Transportation/ Logistics | 73.7 | | | | | |

| VERALL RANK | COMPANY | SECTOR | OVERALL SCORE | CUSTOMER | EMPLOYEE | INNOVATION | SOCIAL | FINANCE |
|---|---|---|---|---|---|---|---|---|
| 21 | Colgate-Palmolive Co. | Consumer Goods | 73.6 | | ★★★★★ | ★★★★ | ★★★★★ | ★★★★★ |
| 22 | Adobe Systems Inc. | Technology | 72.5 | | ★★★★★ | ★★★★ | ★★★★★ | ★★★★★ |
| 23 | Facebook Inc. | Technology | 72.1 | | ★★★★★ | ★★★★★ | ★★★ | ★★★★★ |
| 23 | Jones Lang LaSalle Inc. | Real Estate/ Construction | 72.1 | | ★★★★ | ★★★★★ | ★★★★★ | ★★★ |
| 23 | Merck & Co. | Health Care/ Life Sciences | 72.1 | | ★★★★ | ★★★★★ | ★★★★★ | ★★★ |
| 23 | Wal-Mart Stores Inc. | Retail/Wholesale | 72.1 | | ★★ | ★★★★★ | ★★★★ | ★★★★★ |
| 27 | Exxon Mobil Corp. | Energy | 71.7 | | ★★★★ | ★★★★★ | ★★★★ | ★★★★ |
| 27 | JPMorgan Chase & Co. | Financial Services | 71.7 | | ★★★★ | ★★★★★ | ★★★★★ | ★★★★★ |
| 29 | Lockheed Martin Corp. | Industrial Goods | 71.3 | | ★★★ | ★★★★★ | ★★★★ | ★★★★★ |

| OVERALL RANK | COMPANY | SECTOR | OVERALL SCORE | CUS |
|---|---|---|---|---|
| ) | Intuit Inc. | Technology | | |

| OVERALL RANK | COMPANY | SECTOR | OVERALL SCORE | EMPLOYEE | INNOVATION | SOCIAL | FINANCE |
|---|---|---|---|---|---|---|---|
| 1 | Kimberly-Clark Corp. | Consumer Goods | 70.9 | ★★★★ | ★★★ | ★★★★★ | ★★★★★ |
| 2 | Pfizer Inc. | Health Care/ Life Sciences | 70.5 | ★★★★ | ★★★★ | ★★★★★ | ★★★★★ |
| 3 | Texas Instruments Inc. | Technology | 70.0 | ★★★★★ | ★★★ | ★★★★★ | ★★★★★ |
| 4 | Boeing Co. | Industrial Goods | 69.9 | ★★★★ | ★★★★★ | ★★★★ | ★★★★★ |
| 5 | Hershey Co. | Consumer Goods | 69.9 | ★★★ | ★★★★ | ★★★★ | ★★★★★ |
| 6 | Marriott International Inc. | Leisure/Arts/ Hospitality | 69.9 | ★★★★ | ★★★★★ | ★★★★ | ★★★★ |
| 7 | Coca-Cola Co. | Consumer Goods | 69.8 | ★★★★ | ★★★★★ | ★★★★ | ★★★ |
| 7 | General Motors Co. | Automotive/ Vehicles | 69.8 | ★★★★ | ★★★★★ | ★★★★ | ★★★★ |
| 9 | Allstate Corp. | Financial Services | 69.6 | ★★★ | ★★★★★ | ★★★★ | ★★★ |
| 9 | Edwards Lifesciences Corp. | Health Care/ Life Sciences | 69 | | | | |

| OVERALL RANK | COMPANY | SECTOR | OVERALL SCORE | EMPLOYEE | INNOVATION | SOCIAL | FINANCE |
|---|---|---|---|---|---|---|---|
| 1 | S&P Global Inc. | Financial Services | 68.5 | ★★★★ | ★★★ | ★★★★★ | ★★★★★ |
| 2 | Ford Motor Co. | Automotive/ Vehicles | 68.4 | ★★★★ | ★★★★★ | ★★★★ | ★★★★ |
| 3 | Medtronic PLC | Health Care/ Life Sciences | 68.0 | ★★★★ | ★★★★★ | ★★★★★ | ★★★ |

| OVERALL RANK | COMPANY | SECTOR | OVERALL SCORE | EMPLOYEE | INNOVATION | SOCIAL | FINANCE |
|---|---|---|---|---|---|---|---|
| 44 | Salesforce.com Inc. | Technology | 67.9 | ★★★★★ | ★★★ | ★★★★ | ★★★ |
| 45 | Verizon Communications Inc. | Telecommunication Services | 67.7 | ★★★★ | ★★★★ | ★★★★★ | ★★★★★ |
| 46 | Brown-Forman Corp. | Consumer Goods | 67.5 | ★★★★★ | ★★★★ | ★★★★ | ★★★★ |
| 47 | Amgen Inc. | Health Care/ Life Sciences | 67.2 | ★★★★ | ★★★★ | ★★★★ | ★★★★ |
| 48 | Walt Disney Co. | Media/ Entertainment | 66.9 | ★★★★ | ★★★★★ | ★★★★ | ★★★★ |
| 49 | Estee Lauder Cos. | Consumer Goods | 66.7 | ★★★★ | ★★★★ | ★★★★ | ★★★★ |
| 50 | AbbVie Inc. | Health Care/ Life Sciences | | | | | |

| OVERALL RANK | COMPANY | SECTOR | OVERALL SCORE | EMPLOYEE | INNOVATION | SOCIAL | FINANCE |
|---|---|---|---|---|---|---|---|
| 50 | Applied Materials Inc. | Technology | 66.6 | ★★★★ | ★★★ | ★★★★ | ★★★★★ |
| 52 | Eli Lilly & Co. | Health Care/ Life Sciences | 66.5 | ★★★★ | ★★★★ | ★★★★★ | ★★★★ |
| 53 | Mastercard Inc. | Financial Services | 66.1 | ★★★★ | ★★★★ | ★★★★ | ★★★★★ |
| 54 | Visa Inc. | Financial Services | 65.7 | ★★★ | ★★★★ | ★★★★ | ★★★★ |
| 55 | VMware Inc. | Technology | 65.5 | ★★★★★ | ★★★ | ★★★★ | ★★★★ |
| 56 | Oracle Corp. | Technology | 65.4 | ★★★ | ★★★★ | ★★★★★ | ★★★ |
| 57 | Home Depot Inc. | Retail/Wholesale | 65.1 | ★★★ | ★★★★ | ★★★★ | ★★★★★ |
| 58 | Micron Technology Inc. | Technology | 64.9 | ★★★★ | ★★★ | ★★★ | ★★★★★ |
| 59 | Bank of America Corp. | Financial Services | 64.8 | ★★★★ | ★★★★ | ★★★★★ | ★★★★ |

| OVERALL RANK | COMPANY | SECTOR | OVERALL SCORE | EMPLOYEE | INNOVATION | SOCIAL | FINANCE |
|---|---|---|---|---|---|---|---|
|  | Lam Research Corp. | Technology | 64.7 | ★★★★ | ★★★ | ★★★★ | ★★★★★ |
|  | Rockwell Automation Inc. | Industrial Goods | 64.6 | ★★★★ | ★★★ | ★★★★ | ★★★★ |
|  | Best Buy Co. | Retail/Wholesale | 64.5 | ★★★★ | ★★★ | ★★★★★ | ★★★★ |
|  | Celgene Corp. | Health Care/Life Sciences | 64.2 | ★★★★ | ★★★ | ★★★★ | ★★★★ |
|  | Molson Coors Brewing Co. | Consumer Goods | 64.1 | ★★★★ | ★★★★ | ★★★★ | ★★ |
|  | American Express Co. | Financial Services | 63.9 | ★★★★ | ★★★★★ | ★★★★ | ★★★ |
|  | Hormel Foods Corp. | Consumer Goods | 63.9 | ★★★★ | ★★★ | ★★★★ | ★★★ |
|  | AT&T Inc. | Telecommunication Services | 63.8 | ★★★ | ★★★★ | ★★★★ | ★★★★★ |
|  | Eaton Corp. | Business/Consumer Services | 63.8 | ★★★★ | ★★★ | ★★★★★ | ★★★ |
|  | Altria Group Inc. | Consumer Goods | 63.7 | ★★★★ | ★★★★ | ★★★★ | ★★★★★ |
|  | American Airlines Group Inc. | Transportation/Logistics | 63.7 | ★★★★ | ★★★★★ | ★★★ |  |

- **Other sources to identify potential good quality companies**: For UK investors, the key is to read different articles, news papers and journals such as the **Sunday Times, Morning Star, Shares Magazine and Bloomberg to find out similar rankings for top UK companies and their rankings as a starting point for your research**.

- Then you can chose any **company of interest**, carry out a rigorous research to know if it **has the characteristics of a good quality/top managed company, and why you should buy its stock or not, then check its stock price, performance and make your investment decision.**

## *But are top managed companies good investments?*

- I believe the best way we can answer is by analysing how **theory and practice [ experience]** relates to this question.

- After your analysis, then you can decide if **"top managed companies are good investments or not"**

- First let us analyse the theory behind this question **using an article from the Druker Institute of Management which was published in the Wall Street Journal**

- The article below from Wall Street Journal will give you the theoretical background whether **top managed companies are good investments.**

- Please turn over to the next page and read the article.

# "Are Top-Managed Companies a Good Investment?"

Whether identifying well-run companies can give an investor an edge is uncertain. ILLUSTRATION: STEPHANIE DALTON COWAN FOR THE WALL STREET JOURNAL

*By*
*Ken Brown*
Updated Dec. 5, 2017 3:39 p.m. ET

*Peter Drucker is a legend among management consultants. But can he pick stocks?*

*The late Mr. Drucker built his legacy telling executives to focus on "doing the right things well." That advice has been distilled into the Management Top 250 ranking of the most effectively managed U.S. companies. Next they will be turned into an investment product to see whether Mr. Drucker's philosophy can make money for investors.*

*The Drucker Institute, a research and consulting firm that aims to spread Mr. Drucker's views, is planning to launch an exchange-traded fund that will buy shares of companies that score best on factors like customer satisfaction and innovation. These squishy subjects tend to be hard to grasp for spreadsheet-focused analysts, and the institute aims to show that companies that score high on these factors can beat the market.*

*The logic is simple: Well-run companies should perform well financially, and that should drive their stocks higher. The first part of that idea—that good management leads to higher profits—is generally true, especially relative to competitors in a company's industry.*

*Whether identifying well-run companies can give an investor an edge in the market is iffier. The top scorers in the Drucker data are Amazon.comInc., AMZN +3.96% AppleInc. AAPL +1.82% and Google parent Alphabet Inc., which collectively are up an average of 46% in the past 12 months and are worth $2.1 trillion. It feels like investors, without Mr. Drucker's help, have already figured out these are great companies.*

- *Consumer-Goods Firms Shine in Financial Category*

*But first the positives. The data is an impressive collection of five years of numbers on 37 topics from a wide range of sources, from employee surveys on their pay and job satisfaction to tallies of patents and trademarks, which help determine a company's innovation score. The institute believes that collectively these add up to Mr. Drucker's philosophy. Laying out this kind of data on what are normally considered qualitative factors should be valuable to all investors.*

## MORE IN LEADERSHIP

More important, the institute has connected this nonfinancial data to the companies' financial performance. "What we know now is the intangibles do drive financial performance higher," says Rick Wartzman, director of the KH Moon Center for a Functioning Society, which is part of the Drucker Institute. Specifically, the institute says that when these intangibles improve, they generate a more modest boost in financial performance within two years.

### More positives, and questions

The Drucker data is a gold mine for investors looking to judge a company on its environmental, social and governance performance, criteria that drive an increasing amount of institutional money. There is something of a land rush among companies such as MSCI and Standard & Poor's to supply this kind of data, but Drucker goes deeper, especially on how well a company is run, which falls under governance.

This makes sense. Mr. Drucker was always concerned with the role of business in society, believing a company is responsible for everything and everyone it touches. This requires companies to be well-managed, and it penalizes companies that cut corners in pursuit of short-term profits.

Another positive in the data is that the five main groups of data—financial strength, social responsibility, innovation, customer satisfaction, and employee engagement and development—are correlated with one another. The institute is doing more work on causality—is innovation the thing that drives financial performance, for instance, or, does employee pay matter to customer satisfaction?

The institute's success or failure will depend in part on the quality of its analysis, but also whether it is telling investors anything new. The top of the list is filled with the usual suspects of most admired companies— Procter & Gamble , PG -0.84% Nike, NKE +0.05% Intel , Exxon Mobil , XOM +0.59%Southwest AirlinesLUV +1.29% and StarbucksSBUX -0.15% among them. Yet the performance of those companies' shares has been mixed, largely because of downturns in their industries, something that the Drucker data doesn't capture. The theory is these companies will perform better when the industries turn around, though that is hard to judge.

For example, Procter & Gamble shares are flat for the past three years, in part because of new competitors that have bruised its cash-cow Gillette brand. P&G, ranked No. 6 overall, scores high on innovation, though it was blindsided by upstarts like Dollar Shave Club and Harry's Razors. And the consumer-goods maker is scored extra high on governance, yet its management is embroiled in an embarrassing and expensive fight to keep an activist investor off its board.

## Mixed results

The potentially more interesting list is of companies that have improved their share performance under the Drucker criteria, including chip maker Nvidia ,NVDA +3.22% up sixfold in the past two years, and steelmaker Steel Dynamics, STLD +1.58% which has more than doubled.

The question is whether the data would have gotten investors into a stock quick enough to capture the gains. And, of course, nothing is certain. Other companies that have shown big improvement in the Drucker data, including Discover Financial Services and Southwest Airlines , have lagged behind the market, with shares of some names down the list positively bombing.

*The institute hopes to launch the ETF based on Drucker's top performers next year. Owning a basket of its top-rated companies may be better than using the data to pick individual stocks.*

*But the market moves fast, and the risk is that the Drucker ETF could be left behind" Mr. Brown is The Wall Street Journal's Heard on the Street editor, based in New York. He can be reached at ken.brown@wsj.com.*

## CHAPTER 8: APPLICATION OF THEORY – PRACTICE [EXPERIENCE]

- To apply theory, we will look at the portfolio of 3 different investors who built their portfolio with the top 10 managed companies from the list published by the Drucker Institute of Management

- **80%** of their portfolio were built from the list of top managed companies at **different time periods**.

- Let us call those **Investor, 1, 2 and 3.**

- **Investor 1 invested £13,457** on the **12ᵗʰ October 2018** in her **SIPP [Self Invested Personal Pension]** portfolio made up **mostly of top managed companies**, today, the **18/06/2019**, at the point of writing this book, her portfolio has returned **£15,396**. This means her portfolio is up by **14.4%. Similarly, she invested a total of £2770 in August 2017 in her share dealing account, not a lump sum but different amounts of £2000, £100, £120, £500 and £50 at different intervals. Today her portfolio worth £3214 i.e. 22.41%**

- **Investor 2** invested **£2300 on 4ᵗʰ of March 2019 in her Stocks and Shares ISA account**, today the **18/06/2019**, her portfolio has increased to **£2741.92**. giving a total portfolio return of **19.21%. Initially, she credited her account with £2300 as a lump sum.**

- **Investor 3** started investing **in April 2017**, and funded her Shares Dealing account **regularly** with different amounts such as **£100, £50, £20** based on what she can afford. Note she skipped some months without funding her account because she could not afford to. **Once she bought her stocks, she never sold any of them.** Today her portfolio is **up 31.35%**

### Analysis of the 3 portfolio Performance

- First we can see that all **3 portfolios, 80% of which consists of top managed companies published above, have performed well** with capital appreciation of **14.4%, 22.41%/19.21% and 31.35%**, respecticely, although the investments were made at different time periods i.e. **9 months, 3 months and more than 2 years ago,** respectively.

- The individual performances of **these top managed companies** in the list: **Apple, Facebook, Amazon, Johnson and Johson, Microsoft, Visa etc** has been very good too in **all 3 portfolios [ please check figures 21, 22, 23 and 34 below],**

- Investor 3's portfolio returns held for **over 2 years has the best performance i.e. 31.35%. She** funded her account and bought shares regularly, with different amounts based on how much she can afford. Similarly **investor 1s's sharedealing account held over 2 years is up 22.14%.**

- Their portfolios have performed better **for 3 reasons: primarily they have invested/held shares of top managed companies in their SIPP AND share dealing account portfolio for longer periods than investor 2,**

- Hence, investor 1 and 3 have taken advantage **of compound interest [earning interest on interest] and dividend reinvestment on their stock performance more than investor 2.**

- Remember we talked about **time value of money and compound interest earlier. The longer you hold a stock which is increasing in value and reinvest your dividends,** the better your returns [Microsoft's performance in investor 3's portfolio confirms that– 1st stock investor 3 bought in her portfolio which has increased by 65% over 2 years.

- Secondly, since investor 3 did not buy and sell shares frequently, **meaning her transaction costs was much lower than Investor 1 and 2, in effect reducing the returns of investment 1 and 2 who traded regularly.**

- **This explains why Investor 3's portfolio has the best performance, of about 31%, compared to Investor 1 and 2**

- So if you intend to trade regularly, keep an eye on your transaction costs because it reduces profits made i.e. cost of buying and selling shares.

- Therefore, based on this study, I can conclude from the information above that top **managed companies are good investments for the most part, would you?**

- **The decision is yours to make after analysing the information above. Only then can you decide whether top managed companies are top quality companies, hence if they make good investments or not.**

*Performance figures of the 3 investor's portfolio*

# INVESTOR 1 – INDIVIDUAL STOCK PERFORMANCE IN SIPP PORTFOLIO

Figure 21

## INVESTOR 1- OVERALL SIPP AND SHARE DEALING ACCOUNT PORTFOLIO PERFORMANCE

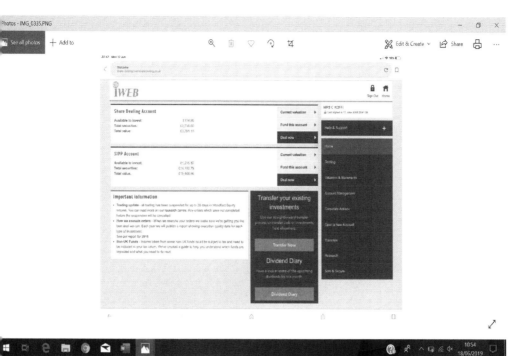

Figure 22

# INVESTOR 2 – OVERALL STOCKS AND SHARES ISA PORTFOLIO PERFORMANCE

Figure 23

# INVESTOR 2 - INDIVIDUAL STOCKS PERFORMANCE IN STOCK AND SHARES PORTFOLIO -figure 24

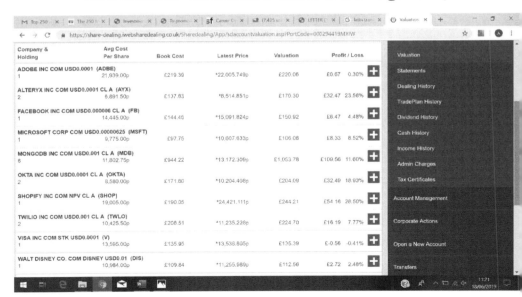

# INVESTOR 3 – OVERALL PORTFOLIO, AND INDIVIDUAL STOCK PERFORMANCE: figure 25

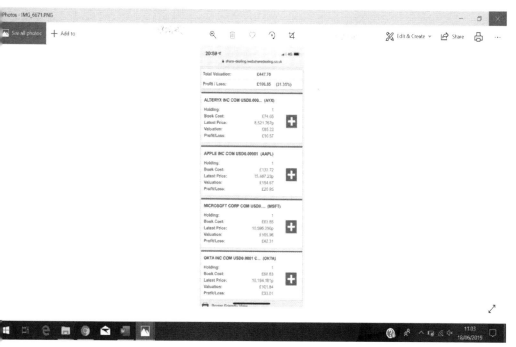

*"First step in making money  - don't lose money"*

*Warren Buffet*

## CHAPTER 9: HOW TO MANAGE YOUR PORTFOLIO, DIVERSIFICATION, WHEN TO BUY AND SELL

- o According to Warren Buffet, **the first step in making money in the market is not to lose money,** hence the need to manage your portfolio well.

- Similarly, William O'Neil [a legendary investor] advises that as an investor you should **aim to lose the least amount of money possible when you are not right.**

- **WHEN TO SELL**: If a stock drops by 8%, O'Neil advises to "Sell" to reduce your losses. For example, if you invested £1000 or $1000 in Apple and lost 8%, this means you have lost £80 of your money.

- **O'Neil** advises us to Sell the stock, **but the choice is yours, because a positive news may lead to an increase of 10% in Apple stocks the next day,** cancelling your losses and increasing the value of your investments

- For example, **my Apple stock value is down by 10%, I decided to stay invested because I believe from research that Apple is a top quality company and the amount I have invested in Apple is not a lot.** Perhaps O'Neil's advice really applies in cases where you are dealing with large sums of money like millions of pounds because 8% loss on £100 investment is £8 but on £1 million is £80,000 which is a lot. **Hence I can understand why one will have sell at 8% in that situation.**

- An alternative - is to reduce your losses is by **selling a fraction of your shares of the company** and **channel the funds to stocks that are doing well.**

- However, if your stock value has increased **by 20%, sell and keep the profits.** But, again it all depends on you the investor because you may want to make the **most of compound interest** by not selling.

- Sometimes I decide to cash out at 10% or 13% because I am comfortable with it or want to use my profit for something else e.g. 10% of £1000 or $1000 investment in a stock is £100 or $100, which is a decent amount of money to use for food shopping.

- **NOTE: From experience, I believe the right balance is to cash out some of your profits, say 80% and leaving some, say 20%. This limits the risk of losing all your profits in case the market goes down due to a crash, but at the same time taking advantage of the effect of compound interest**

- **Diversify or not?** So, you may want to enjoy the fruits of your labour by cashing out and leaving the capital or invest the profit in another stock to make more profit and **diversify your portfolio to reduce risks of putting all your "eggs" in one basket**.

- **Diversification is one key strategy in reducing risks and minimising losses. It simply means instead of investing all your money say £10,000 in one stock, say, Amazon, you rather invest 10 different top quality stocks**

- **STOP-LOSS TOOL**: Use the "Stop-Loss" tool on your trading platform to control your loss, if the platform has one.

- This system helps you to place an order in your portfolio to sell shares of a stock if losses reach a certain target e.g. **to "automatically sell Apple stocks if losses hit 8 % or "Sell when the stock has gained by 10% or 20%.**

- **This is very important**. Why? Experience shows in most cases you **will forget to carry out this process of buying or selling, manually most of the time** when you need to, because you are busy with something else.

- **Consequently, you may earn up losing more money than you would have wanted to, when the stock price is sinking.**

- **TRANSACTION COSTS:** Having said that, too much buying and selling increases your transaction costs. So, it is very important to reduce your losses by **reducing the rate at which you buy or sell**

- From my experience or viewpoint, owning good quality stocks of top managed companies for a long time **is critical in making sustainable profits, money or passive income - because a good company remains the same in good and bad times**.

- The case study below, published recently by Forbes magazine, **shows how one of the greatest investors you have never heard of "Beat the odds to become a billionaire by investing mostly in the stock market**

# *The Greatest Investor You've Never Heard Of: An Optometrist Who Beat The Odds To Become A Billionaire*

## *Madeline Berg - Forbes*

**It's 9 p.m. on the last Saturday night** *of the 2018 Art Basel in Miami Beach. On the first floor of the palatial Versace mansion, the well-dressed and well-Botoxed are dancing to remixes of Michael Jackson's "Beat It" and posing for Instagram by the mosaic-tiled emerald pool.*

*Upstairs, in a VIP room decorated in a mélange of styles that marry classical Greek and Roman touches, a well-dressed septuagenarian named Herbert Wertheim is sitting in front of a plate of smoked-salmon toast topped with gold leaf and shaved truffles, and scrolling through photos on his iPhone—scenes from what could only be described as a wonderful life. There are fan photos of him cooking pasta fagioli with Martha Stewart, on the slopes with Buzz Aldrin and fishing in Antarctica. There are many with his wife of 49 years, Nicole, on the luxurious World Residences at Sea, a yacht where the Wertheims now live part of each year. He calls these extracurricular activities "Herbie time."*

*If it weren't for his trademark bright-red fedora, Wertheim, who is an optometrist and small businessman, would look like the typical senior living it up in South Florida.*

*But Wertheim, 79, has no need for early-bird specials. What the **photos [please see photos by clicking on link below]** don't reveal is that Dr. Herbie, as he is known to friends, is a **self-made billionaire worth $2.3 billion by Forbes' reckoning—not including the $100 million he has donated to Florida's public universities. His fortune comes not from some flash of entrepreneurial brilliance or dogged devotion to career, but from a lifetime of prudent do-it-yourself buy-and-hold investing.***

Herb Wertheim may be the greatest individual investor the world has never heard of, and he has the Fidelity statements to prove it. Leafing through printouts he has brought to a meeting, **you can see hundreds of millions of dollars in stocks like Apple and Microsoft, purchased decades ago during their IPOs. An $800 million-plus position in Heico, a $1.8 billion (revenue) airplane-parts manufacturer, dates to 1992. There are dozens of other holdings, ranging from GE and Google to BP and Bank of America. If there's a common theme to Wertheim's investing, it's a preference for industry and technology companies and dividend payers. His financial success—and the fantastic life his portfolio has afforded his family—is a testament to the power of compounding as well as to the resilience of American innovation over the half-century.**

"My thing is," Wertheim says as he reflects on his long career, "I wanted to be able to have free time. To me, having time is the most precious thing."

**Born in Philadelphia at the end of the Great Depression,** Wertheim is the son of Jewish immigrants who fled Nazi Germany. In 1945 his parents moved to Hollywood, Florida, and lived in an apartment above the family's bakery. A dyslexic, Wertheim struggled in school and soon found himself skipping class.

"In those days, they just called you dumb," he remembers. "I would sit in the corner sometimes with a dunce cap on."

**"My thing is I wanted to be able to have free time. To me, having time is the most precious thing."**

During his teens, in the 1950s, an abusive father prompted Wertheim to run away periodically. He spent much of his time hanging around with the local Seminole Indians, hunting and fishing in the Everglades and selling game, like frog legs, to locals. He also hitchhiked around Florida picking oranges and grapefruits. Eventually, his parents had enough. At age 16 he stood in front of a judge facing truancy charges. Lucky for Wertheim, the judge took pity on him, offering him a choice between the U.S. Navy and state reformatory. Wertheim enlisted in 1956 and was stationed in San Diego. He was only 17.

"That's where my life changed," he says. "They give you tests all the time to see how smart you are, and out of 135 in our class, I think I was in the top—especially in the areas of mechanics and organization."

With a newfound confidence, Wertheim studied physics and chemistry in the Navy before working in naval aviation. This is about the time Wertheim began investing in stocks. It was the Cold War, the military-industrial complex was humming and American industry was on the move. The Dow Jones Industrial Average had finally recovered from the losses it suffered more than two decades before during the Crash of 1929, and aerospace stocks were leading the market. Wertheim made his first investment at 18, using his Navy stipend to buy stock in Lear Jet, which at the time was known for making aviation products during WWII. Wertheim met its founder, Bill Lear, during a visit to a Sikorsky Aircraft factory in Connecticut, where the Navy's S58 helicopters were manufactured. Wertheim was attracted to Lear's inventions, like the first auto-pilot systems. (Later, the company would invent the 8-track tape and pioneer the business-jet market.)

**"You take what you earn with the sweat of your brow, then you take a percentage of that and you invest it in other people's labor," Wertheim says of his near-religious devotion to tithing his wages into the stock market.**

Once out of the Navy, Wertheim sold encyclopedias door-to-door before attending Brevard Community College and then the University of Florida, where he studied engineering but never graduated. In addition to taking classes, he worked for NASA—then in its first few years—in a division that improved instrumentation for manned flights. This fueled an interest in the eye and instruments optimized for vision.

**His fortune comes not from some flash of entrepreneurial brilliance but from a lifetime of prudent buy-and-hold investing.**

In 1963 he received a scholarship to attend the Southern College of Optometry in Memphis and after graduation opened up a practice in South Florida. For 12 years he toiled away, seeing patients who were mostly working-class and who sometimes paid their bills with bushels of mangoes and avocados. Wertheim spent his evenings tinkering on inventions, and in 1969, he invented an eyeglass tint for plastic lenses that would filter out and absorb dangerous UV rays, helping to prevent cataracts.

The Vietnam War was under way, and plastics had become the material of choice for eyeglasses and sunglasses. Demand for Wertheim's tint grew, and he sold it in a royalty deal for $22,000. But because of contractual breaches, the royalties never materialized.

So in 1970 Wertheim decided to get more serious about his inventions and set up a new company, Brain Power Inc. He founded it as a technology consulting firm, but Wertheim soon returned to his habit of researching and tinkering, developing tints, dyes and other technologies for eyewear.

A year later he concocted one of the world's first neutralizers, a chemical that restored lenses back to their original clear state. This meant opticians no longer needed to carry large inventories of different-colored lenses or dispose of lenses that were improperly tinted. "I was still seeing patients, I had a little lab," recalls Wertheim with a smile. He showed his wife a coffee can containing his chemical concoction and said, 'Nicole, what's in this can is going to make us millionaires.'"

Wertheim occasionally lectures on engineering at Florida International University.

It did. Between that chemical and the numerous other products Wertheim invented for lenses—some tints for aesthetics, others to help ease the symptoms of neurological disorders like epilepsy and still others to improve UV protection—BPI became one of the world's largest manufacturers of optical tints, selling to companies like Bausch & Lomb, Zeiss and Polaroid. The company also began making lab equipment, cleaners and accessories for opticians, optometrists and ophthalmologists. Today BPI has more than 100 patents and copyrights in the area of optics, 49 employees and annual revenues of about $25 million.

In less than two decades, Wertheim had gone from ne'er-do-well to inventor and entrepreneur. BPI never achieved hypergrowth, but it currently has a net income of about $10 million a year, according to Wertheim, more than enough to feed his passion for investing and the good life.

*"I didn't want to have a big business," he says. "But today, I have a 5 or a 6 or an 8 billion-dollar corporation, each of which I own 10% of."*

With BPI cash flowing into Wertheim's brokerage account, he went to work buying stocks and honing a strategy that can best be described as a mix of Warren Buffett and Peter Lynch, with a touch of Jack Bogle, given that he dislikes fees and primarily uses two discounters, Fidelity and Schwab, to manage his massive portfolio.

With Lear Jet (later known as Lear Siegler) in the late 1950s, for example, Wertheim was practicing "invest in what you know," the strategy popularized by the famous Fidelity Magellan fund manager Peter Lynch in his 1989 book One Up on Wall Street. Lynch told readers to use their specialized knowledge or experience to gain an edge in their investments.

In less than two decades, Wertheim had gone from ne'er-do-well to inventor and entrepreneur.

## How Dr. Herbert Wertheim Got His Red Hat | 1:10

Instead of concentrating on the metrics in financial statements, Wertheim is devoted to reading patents and spends two six-hour blocks each week poring over technical tomes. "What's more important to me is, what is your intellectual capital to be able to grow?" Thanks to his engineering background, the technical nature of optometry and his experience as an inventor, the patent library is Wertheim's comfort zone. Stocks he invested in based on their impressive patent portfolios include IBM, 3M and Intel.

Like Warren Buffett, Wertheim believes firmly in doubling down when his high-conviction picks go against him. He says that if you put your faith in a company's intellectual property, it doesn't matter too much if the market goes south for a bit—the product, he believes, has lasting value.

"If you like something at $13 a share, you should like it at $12, $11 or $10 a share," Wertheim says. "If a stock continues to go down, and you believe in it and did your research, then you buy more. You are actually getting a better deal." Whenever possible, he adds, dividends are useful in cushioning the pain of stocks that drift down or go sideways.

"My goal is to buy and almost never sell," he says, parroting a Buffettism. "I let it appreciate as much as it can and use the dividends to move forward." In this way Wertheim, like the Oracle of Omaha, seldom reinvests dividends but instead uses the cash flow from his portfolio to either fund his lifestyle or make new investments.

Wertheim points to Microsoft, a stock he has held since its IPO in 1986. "I knew a lot about computers and had been involved in building them," he says. BPI had been using Apple IIe's, but after Microsoft released its Windows operating system in 1985, Wertheim became convinced it would be a winner. "Only Microsoft had an operating system that could compete with Apple," he recalls. The Microsoft shares he bought during the IPO, which have been paying dividends since 2003, are now worth more than $160 million. His 1.25 million shares of Apple, some purchased during its 1980 IPO and some when the stock was languishing at $10 in the 1990s, are worth $195 million.

# COMPOUNDING: THE MOST POWERFUL FORCE

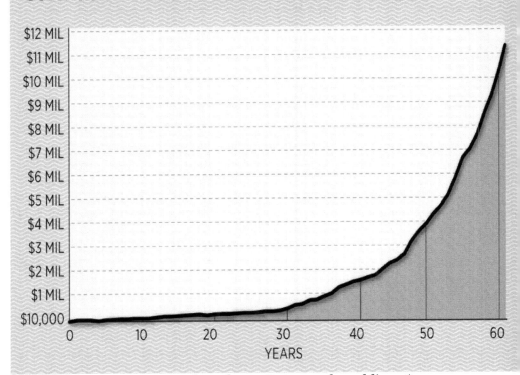

*Wertheim's returns are miraculous. But merely adding $200 per month to an initial $10,000 in the stock market over the past 61 years would have produced an $11 million portfolio.*
*SOURCE: INVESTOR.GOV*

Not all of the hundreds of stocks he has owned have fared so well. He invested big in Blackberry. "I believed in the new management and the recovery story," says Wertheim, who will generally sell if a position reverses on him by 25%. "I watched substantial profits disappear month after month until I decided enough was enough."

**Wertheim sometimes uses leverage, but mostly in a limited way when buying high-yielding stocks. "By using the dividends to offset [the cost of] margin interest, the government is helping you increase your portfolio value," he explains, noting that margin interest is tax deductible up to the amount of ordinary income.**

*"If you like something at $13 a share, you should like it at $12, $11 or $10 a share,"* Wertheim says. *"If a stock continues to go down, and you believe in it and did your research, then you buy more."*

But in 1982 Wertheim got caught in a margin call after Federal Reserve Chairman Paul Volcker raised the federal funds rate from 12% to 20% and the market sank 20%. The episode cost him $50 million and taught Wertheim a valuable lesson about the dangers of leverage and mark-to-market accounting. Like most other active investors, Wertheim strives for tax efficiency. In order to harvest tax losses in his portfolio, he doubles down on his losers to avoid the IRS' wash-sale penalties. "If I have a large loss in a stock I like," he says, "I will purchase more, usually twice to three times the original purchase, and wait the 30 days to sell the original position and book the tax loss."

As with Buffett, Wertheim says finding companies with strong management has been key to his success. A great example of this is Heico, a family-run aerospace and electronics company based in Wertheim's hometown, Hollywood, Florida.

---

**Wertheim became friendly with Laurans "Larry" Mendelson during the 1970s,** after Wertheim bought a condominium in a building Mendelson owned and docked his boat next to Mendelson's on Coral Gables Waterway. "He has two daughters around the same age as my two sons," Mendelson says. "We got to know each other socially."

A CPA by training, Mendelson was a successful real estate investor who had studied at Columbia Business School under David Dodd, co-author with Benjamin Graham of the seminal book on value investing, Security Analysis. Inspired by the wave of dealmakers getting rich from LBOs in the 1980s, the Mendelsons were looking to find an undervalued, underperforming industrial company to take over.

After they settled on Heico, at the time a small airline-parts maker, Wertheim used his aeronautical knowledge to informally help the family analyze its business and went on to purchase shares of the company—a penny stock priced as low as 33 cents.

**"My goal is to buy and almost never sell."**

"At that time Heico was a disaster, but he came up and understood what we would do to make it a non-disaster," says Mendelson. Heico was making narrow-body jet-engine combustors, which the FAA mandated be replaced on a regular basis after a plane caught fire on a runway in 1985. **Under the Mendelsons, Heico expanded its line of replacement parts, which undercut established original-equipment manufacturers like United Technologies' Pratt & Whitney and GE. After Germany's Lufthansa acquired a minority stake in the company in 1997, airline manufacturers and Wall Street took notice, and its share price rose sixfold to more than $2. But this was just the beginning.** Heico enjoyed a proverbial moat as one of only a few FAA-approved airplane replacement-parts manufacturers. This translated into steadily growing orders as Heico expanded its product mix and as demand for air travel increased. For the last 28 years, Heico's sales have compounded at a rate of 16% per year and its net profits at 19%.

Today, Heico trades for $80, and buy-and-hold Herbie is its largest individual shareholder. His original $5 million investment is worth more than $800 million.

*Clockwise from top: Wertheim with Warren Buffett; on the World in Bordeaux; sightseeing in the North Pole; with his wife, Nicole, in Corsica; examining eyes in Guatemala.*

**As Wertheim enters his 80th year,** Herbie time has become his chief preoccupation. Besides his $16 million oceanfront home in Coral Gables, Wertheim has a 90-acre ranch near Vail, Colorado, a spectacular four-story home overlooking the Thames in London and two sprawling estates in southern California. He spends many winters with his wife and family vacationing aboard The World, the planet's largest luxurious residential ship continuously circumnavigating the globe, where he owns two luxury apartments. Right now, in the middle of February, the Wertheims are somewhere off the coast of Sri Lanka.

A signee of Bill Gates and Warren Buffett's Giving Pledge, Wertheim has committed to giving away at least half his wealth, and he intends the bulk of the donations to go to public education—the very system of which he is a product.

"I would not have achieved the education and opportunities that I have had without the help of our public-university education system," he wrote when he signed the pledge.

Stroll around Florida International University's main campus, just minutes from Wertheim's Coral Gables home, and you can't help but notice buildings emblazoned with his name: the Herbert Wertheim College of Medicine, the Nicole Wertheim College of Nursing & Health Sciences, the Herbert & Nicole Wertheim Performing Arts Center and the Wertheim Conservatory. He has given $50 million to FIU and committed another $50 million to the University of Florida. Last year he pledged $25 million to the University of California, San Diego, to help create a school of public health. Beyond education, Wertheim says he's given to hundreds of domestic and foreign nonprofits, including the Miami Zoo and the Vail, Colorado, public radio station.

The former truant and class dunce still gets giddy when he sees his name on the university buildings, asking passersby to take photos—posing in his signature red hat and new Nikes. At the medical school, he put on a stethoscope, excited to test out the latest medical dummies, which breathe, sweat and even talk. In a room designed to study obstetrics, he tries his hand at an ultrasound machine. At a lab that he helps fund, he is enamored with laser imaging and how it can help measure retinal temperature in the eye. ("I've fallen in love with proteins," he says casually, discussing another eye experiment.) At the FIU performing arts center bearing his name, he suggests adding an outdoor amphitheater: "I think it's time. I'd like to see something big happen."

"He's very inspirational in the way he challenges people to think big and imagine what's possible," says Cammy Abernathy, dean of the Herbert Wertheim College of Engineering at the University of Florida.

**Still, one gets the sense that devoting time to his stock-portfolio provides as much joy for Wertheim as his playful excursions and philanthropies.**

**He recently doubled down on British energy giant BP and now owns over one million shares. But rather than dwell on its sagging, crude-dependent stock chart, he's betting on its hydrogen fuel cells and enjoying its 6% dividend yield while he waits for the company to recover.**

**"They have important intellectual property in that area," he says of the cells, which create electricity by using hydrogen**

*as fuel, a technology Wertheim believes is the future of both air and road transportation. "We're going to move to a hydrogen economy." Contrarian Wertheim also likes the troubled stock of General Electric; he owns over 15 million shares and has been picking up more.*

*He says he is making a long-term bet on GE's intellectual property; the 126-year-old company has more than 179,000 patents and growing. Wertheim is especially jazzed about some patents that involve the 3-D printing of metal engine parts.*

*"You can't look at what their sales are. You can't look at anything. What is the future?" he says emphatically, adding, "They hit an all-time low yesterday, and I'm getting hurt. But I feel very, very comfortable with GE because of their technology."*

*And Wertheim isn't in any rush. Playing the long game is what he does best.*

[Online] Available at: https://www.forbes.com/sites/maddieberg/2019/02/19/the-greatest-investor-youve-never-heard-of-an-optometrist-who-beat-the-odds-to-become-a-billionaire/#5896c7a22e8a.[Accessed on 02/01/2020.

- ARE YOU INSPIRED BY HERBERT'S STORY TO BECOME THE NEXT BILLIONAIRE BY INVESTING IN THE STOCK MARKET?

- IF SO, START NOW, NOT LATER BECAUSE **TIME** WILL PLAY A CRITICAL ROLE IN HELPING YOU TO ACHIEVE THIS GOAL.

**REMEMBER "INSPIRATION WITHOUT ACTION IS MERELY ENTERTAINMENT"**

**GOOD LUCK IN YOUR JOURNEY IN BECOMING A SUCCESSFUL INVESTOR!**

Printed in Great Britain
by Amazon

36454500R00047